# MICHAEL DAVIES

# the Roman Rite Destroyed

## ANGELUS PRESS

2915 FOREST AVENUE,
KANSAS CITY, MISSOURI 64109

**ANGELUS PRESS**
2915 FOREST AVENUE
KANSAS CITY, MISSOURI 64109
PHONE (816) 753-3150
FAX (816) 753-3557
ORDER LINE 1-800-966-7337

ISBN 0-935952-10-1
First published by Augustine Publishing Co., January 1978
Angelus Press First Edition—August 1983
Angelus Press Second Edition, First Printing—February 1992
Angelus Press Second Edition, Second Printing—April 2003

Printed in the United States of America

# CONTENTS

I    Cranks in Authority ................................................................. 3
     *A revolution has taken place–The submissive laity–*
     *Liturgical "doublethink"*

II   An Ecumenical Liturgy ............................................................ 17
     *Lex orandi, lex credendi–Towards a common liturgy–*
     *The Case for the New Mass*

III  A Qualification ...................................................................... 42
     *Minorities can be right–The fort is betrayed*

Appendix .................................................................................... 47
     *The participation of the Protestant observers in the*
     *compilation of the new Catholic liturgical texts*

Notes  ........................................................................................ 51

Index  ........................................................................................ 53

## ILLUSTRATIONS

A Marxist Mass ........................................................................... 8

The Mass of the Eternal Church at Ecône ................................... 25

Paul VI and the Six Protestant Observers .................................. 46

# I
# CRANKS IN AUTHORITY

In 1570 Pope St. Pius V codified the form of Mass then used in Rome and extended its use throughout the Latin rite, with a few carefully specified exceptions. The history of this Mass has already been provided in an earlier pamphlet in this series, *The Tridentine Mass*, and will not be repeated here. Let it suffice to say, in the words of Father Faber, that it is "the most beautiful thing this side of heaven," as near to perfection as anything can be in an imperfect world. The Tridentine Mass is perfect in its form, perfect in the doctrine it enshrines. "If we take the entire service as a whole," wrote Cardinal Wiseman, "it is constructed with the most admirable symmetry, proportioned in its parts with perfect judgement and so exquisitely arranged as to excite and preserve an unbroken interest in the sacred action."[1]

Apart from its continued celebration by a relatively small number of priests who have remained faithful to the Mass of their ordination, this sublime liturgy, this foretaste of heaven on earth, has been destroyed. Those who exercise power in the Church today deny this. Bishops in their pastorals, priests from their pulpits, the Catholic press, the Catholic Information Office, all assure us that what we have been given in place of the Roman Mass is nothing new but that same Mass itself. They insist that there have been no changes of any consequence — the use of the vernacular, a revised lectionary, the Bidding Prayers, lay readers — all are very trivial, all incidental; in fact, there is nothing to be worried about but, on the contrary, something to be welcomed with joy and thanksgiving.[2]

This is totally untrue. There has been a revolution. The form of Mass we knew, the Roman Mass, has been destroyed. Note well that I am not claiming that *the Mass* has been destroyed. The Mass itself must not be confused with any individual Mass rite. There have always been different rites of Mass within the Church; the Slavonic

3

liturgy of the Ukrainians is just as much *the Mass* as the Mass of St. Pius V itself. What I am claiming is that, with the rare exceptions already mentioned, that particular form of Mass which we refer to as the Roman Mass no longer exists, it has been destroyed.

There is no lack of traditionalist testimonies to this fact. As early as May 1969, Msgr. Domenico Celeda, an outspoken young Italian prelate, remarked:

"The gradual destruction of the liturgy is a sad fact already well known. Within less than five years, the 1000-year-old structure of divine worship which throughout the centuries has been known as the *Opus Dei* has been dismantled...Instead, a puerile form of rite has been imposed, noisy, uncouth, and extremely boring. And hypocritically, no notice has been taken of the disturbance and disgust of the faithful...Resounding success has been claimed for it because a proportion of the faithful has been trained to repeat mechanically a succession of phrases which through repetition have already lost their effect."[3]

One of the manifold aspects of the "Spirit of Vatican II" is that once a person has been labelled as a traditionalist nothing he or she might say is accounted as worthy of consideration. Whether what a traditionalist says can be proved to be objectively correct is of no consequence; it is sufficient to label him as a traditionalist to rule him out of court. In order to overcome this obstacle, traditionalists will rarely be quoted in this pamphlet. It will not be difficult to rely mainly upon the testimonies of those who have never been involved with the traditionalist movement to prove that what we have witnessed since Vatican II is not a reform but a revolution. The order that is imposed after a revolution is never the order that existed before. The very purpose of a revolution is to overthrow the existing order. Thus what is used in our churches today is not a reformed version of the Mass of St. Pius V, which was what Vatican II ordered, but a *Novus Ordo Missae*, a *new* Mass, something the Council did not envisage.

Some of the faithful had become anxious about possible changes in the Mass while the Council was still in

4

progress. In a Lenten Pastoral issued in 1964, between the third and fourth sessions, Cardinal Heenan referred to these fears. "Take, for example, changes in Holy Mass. Some of you are quite alarmed. You imagine that everything will be changed and what you have known from childhood will be taken away from you."[4]

These fears proved to be only too justified. By August 1965, Evelyn Waugh issued a public protest and warning. He noted that private representations made through the proper channels were disregarded and that the time had come to speak out "to warn the submissive laity of the dangers impending". Those propagating the theories now being imposed had been "with us in parts of the USA and northern Europe for a generation. We looked on them as harmless cranks who were attempting to devise a charade of second-century habits. We had confidence in the abiding *Romanita* of our Church. Suddenly we find the cranks in authority."[5]

The cranks are in authority, that is it precisely. And it is those who attempt to preserve sanity in the Church who are now portrayed as cranks. The late Archbishop Hallinan of Atlanta (USA) also noted that:

"We have come to the end of an era. What used to be uncharitably called the 'way-out ideas' of the 'way-out litniks' are now universal church law."[6]

## A Revolution has Taken Place

When Pope Paul VI promulgated the new Missal on 3 April, 1969, it was clear that a revolution had taken place. This is conceded with surprising frankness by *The Ampleforth Journal*, a review which is normally dedicated to praising the constantly escalating benefits of the "Conciliar Church".

"Between Maundy Thursday 1969 and Maundy Thursday 1970 a liturgical revolution (evolution, perhaps?) of unprecedented proportions was promulgated and put into effect."[7]

On 15 September, 1969, Cardinal Heenan issued another Pastoral Letter. He explained the reason for the continual changes in the Mass:

"Here is the answer. It would have been foolhardy to introduce the changes all at once. Some enthusiasts said that the bishops were 'dragging their feet'. But it was obviously wiser to change gradually and gently. If all the changes had been introduced together you would have been shocked."

Two French liturgists with an international reputation, experts (*periti*) during the Council and in the vanguard of the new corps of liturgical commissars which has worked to impose the revolution with such ruthlessness since the Council ended, have spoken out with even more frankness than *The Ampleforth Journal*. Father Joseph Gelineau, S.J., is well known as an authority on the liturgy and also for his musical settings of the psalms in the vernacular. In a book published in 1976 he had the integrity to state quite openly that:

"To prevent any misunderstanding, to translate is not to say the same thing with equivalent words. It is to change the formula (*C'est changer la forme*). Now the liturgy is not simply a means of imparting information, a lesson in which nothing matters but the content. It is constituted a symbolic action by formulae (*formes*) with a definite signification. If the formulae change the rite is changed. If a singe element is changed the signification of the whole is modified. Let those who like myself have known and sung a Latin-Gregorian High Mass remember it if they can. Let them compare it with the Mass that we now have. Not only the words, the melodies, and some of the gestures are different. To tell the truth, it is a different liturgy of the Mass (*c'est une autre liturgie de la messe*). This needs to be said without ambiguity: the Roman rite as we knew it no longer exists (*le rite romain tel que nous l'avons connu n'existe plus*). It has been destroyed. (*Il est détruit*). Some walls of the former edifice have fallen while others have changed their appearance, to the extent that it appears today either as a ruin or the partial substructure of a different building."[8]

The second of these experts, Fr. Henri Denis, has written in his latest book (published in 1977) that:

"To claim that everything has changed is quite simply to be honest about what has happened. In some of the debates with traditionalists it has sometimes become the accepted practice to say that nothing has been changed. It would be better far to have the courage to admit that the Church has made important modifications and that she had good reason to do so. Why not acknowledge that religion has changed...?"[9]

As early as 1968, Father Louis Bouyer, another liturgist with an international reputation, recognized that the reform that had been imposed was not simply a betrayal of what the Council Fathers had intended but of the entire liturgical movement of the present century, a turning of the back "deliberately on what Beauduin, Casel, and Pius Parsch had set out to do, and to which I had tried vainly to add some small contribution of my own."[10]

Fr. Bouyer also made the startling (but only too accurate) allegation that:

"Once again, at this point, we must speak plainly: there is practically no liturgy worthy of the name today in the Catholic Church."[11]

In 1975 he expressed himself even more strongly:

"The Catholic liturgy has been overthrown under the pretext of rendering it more compatible with the contemporary outlook (*moeurs sécularisées*) — but in reality to conform it with the buffooneries that the religious orders were induced to impose, whether they liked it or not, upon the other clergy. We don't have to wait for the result: a sudden decline in religious practice, varying between twenty and forty per cent among those who were practicing Catholics...those who weren't have not displayed even a trace of interest in this pseudo-missionary liturgy, particularly the young whom they had deluded themselves into thinking they would win over with their clowning."[12]

While it remains true that the objectionable features of the new Mass would still have been objectionable even if it had been a pastoral success with a widespread increase in Mass attendance, it is worth emphasizing that

# A MARXIST MASS

The consecration of the wine at a sacrilegious Mass being celebrated in a room at the Church of St. Peter the Apostle, Montreal, Canada, 12 September 1976.

This "Mass" was concelebrated by several Catholic priests and a Protestant minister, all in lay dress. Only the prayers for the consecration of the bread and wine were preserved, the hosts were great chunks of bread, the wine was consecrated in glasses passed from hand to hand, and some of the verses in the text contained an open incitement in favour of Communism. The screen behind the celebrants had just shown a film with dialogue in support of the Marxist Freemason, ex-President Allende of Chile. The Archbishop of Montreal did not reply to protests at this profanation. (Reproduced with permission from *Crusade for a Christian Civilization*, April 1977, pp.21ff.)

the reform has been a pastoral disaster. One recent survey has put the decline in Mass attendance in France at 66%; in Holland it is 54%; in the USA, 30%; in England and Wales (where the reform has been muted in comparison with most countries), 16% — in comparison with an annual increase before the "renewal".[13]

The failure of gimmicks to make any lasting impact upon the young has been noted by priests in a number of countries. No one could be more liberal or less traditionally minded than America's Father Andrew Greeley. He comments:

"As one student said to me, 'The last place in the world to which I'd go to encounter the sacred is my church.' Some clergy and some churches, noting that there is no one under 25 around any more, decide that something must be done, that the church must 'get with it'.

"So the clergy let their hair go long, use words like 'ripoff', smoke grass, take baths once a week, sleep with a guitar and, like man, really swing. The churches have rock masses, and dancers in skimpy clothes cavorting around the sanctuary, and praise 'Superstar' and Lenny Berstein's phony religious music.

"But it doesn't seem to work. Somehow, the young are not attracted by clerics who act like drug freaks and churches that try to substitute for the local coffee shop or to do the Woodstock thing."[14]

In England, Father Michael Richards, who is editor of the extremely liberal and anti-traditionalist *Clergy Review*, complained that the bishops had handed over their mission to "a few second-rank, rootless technicians who now want to extend their power beyond the field of translations to the field of pastoral and missionary application". He adds that until these "liturgical bookworms and tradesmen" are driven "back to their studies and their counting houses...the Mass as we have it in English will remain where it has descended, at the level of the bingo hall, the quiz program and the lucky dip. I have often thought, but hesitated to believe, that many of those set over us take their public for fools. Now I begin to believe it. And I shall share their view if the Catholic public accepts this nonsense much longer."[15]

Unfortunately, the majority of Catholics have now accepted so much that they would probably accept anything — and those who find that they have had enough are far more likely to join the ninety plus per cent of the British people who do not worship on Sundays than to find their way to a Tridentine Mass centre. Paradoxically, the Bishops seem far more alarmed at the fact that a few thousand Catholics have chosen to worship God in the traditional manner each Sunday than that tens of thousands are choosing not to worship Him at all.

## The Submissive Laity

The fact that Evelyn Waugh's warning to "the submissive laity" went unheeded is not really surprising. In Britain, in particular, submissiveness had been the characteristic of the good Catholic. In practice, it had worked admirably. For well over a century a series of firm, orthodox Popes had given excellent guidance and excellent leadership — they expected their teaching to be accepted and ensured that it was. The Bishops passed on the Vatican directives to the clergy, and the clergy transmitted them to the laity. The essence of Catholicism appeared to be accepting the directives of the person one scale up in a clearly defined hierarchy. The possibility that wrong or harmful instructions could come from above, or what should be done if this happened, was never considered precisely because it never did happen.

However, there was a small avant-garde, the cranks referred to by Evelyn Waugh, and this number was increased by the atmosphere generated by the Council. But these were precisely the type of people who would certainly welcome liturgical changes. Anything new, anything ecumenical, anything "with-it" was obligatory in their view. Thus the one group which was making a point of not accepting Vatican directives unquestioningly (such as *Humanae Vitae*, for example) would have only one complaint about the liturgical reforms, namely that they were not radical enough. The more orthodox Catholics could be relied upon to accept, if not to welcome, any changes imposed with the authority of the Pope. The latest innovation in Britain and the U.S.A., is the introduction of Communion in the hand. Before its introduction it is doubtful whether even one per cent of Mass-goers wanted it, but now that it is here it is doubtful if more than a few per cent will go the extent of actually opposing it. Revolutionaries do not need massive support to succeed, they only require minimal opposition.

It is also a fact of life that the average man in the street or man in the pew does not think very deeply about such matters as politics or religion. * The percentage of adults who have actually read a book about politics or religion is very small indeed. They are thus very susceptible to propaganda, particularly from those they consider to be experts. The imposition of the new liturgy was accompanied by a sustained barrage of propaganda from the pulpit and the Catholic press. The faithful were told that these changes were for their good and for the good of the Church; that they would welcome and enjoy them; that, in fact, they had been clamoring for them for decades; and that, to clinch the matter, the unquestioning acceptance of these changes would be the acid test of their loyalty to the Pope. The minority of Catholics, often converts, who recognized the dangers implicit in the changes, had no opportunity of presenting their case. A few letters did get into the Catholic and secular press but their effect, in comparison with the sustained barrage of propaganda from the official media, the pulpit in particular, was minimal. The average reaction was: "Father says it's good for me so it must be good for me." It is a fundamental axiom of the advertising world that if you tell people they enjoy something often enough, they will enjoy it — and now there is certainly a large proportion of Mass-goers who

---

\*     In his monumental work, *The Great Terror*, Robert Conquest notes that "...it was one of Stalin's most constant principles that most minds are not critical." (Pelican edition, p. 740.).

have convinced themselves that they do like the changes and would certainly object to any attempt to reverse the process. Thus there is a ready audience for the type of propaganda churned out to justify Communion in the hand: that it is more mature, adult, in keeping with the dignity of modern man.

It is also important to stress the effect of introducing the revolution by stages. This was precisely the policy pursued by Cranmer who, at the beginning of his liturgical revolution, avoided any drastic changes "which would needlessly provoke the conservatives and stiffen the attitude of that large class of men who, rightly handled, could be brought to acquiesce in ambiguity and interim measures."[16]

I have gone into the manner in which Cranmer imposed his changes in considerable detail in *Cranmer's Godly Order* I will not repeat the evidence here beyond citing the four stages of his revolution, the first three of which have already been repeated during the current reform.

"*Stage one* was to have certain portions of the unchanged traditional Mass in the vernacular. *Stage two* was to introduce new material into the old Mass, none of which would be specifically heretical. *Stage three* was to replace the old Mass with a vernacular Communion service which, once more, was not specifically heretical. *Stage four* was to replace this service with a specifically Protestant one."[17]

By this technique the clergy and people became accustomed to change. The idea that the Mass couldn't be changed was replaced with the recognition that it could — and each new change that was accepted led to a more ready acceptance of the next. The final result was that the majority of clergy and people were prepared to accept, or at least not to resist, any change.

The type of propaganda in favor of the present revolution, which I have already cited, was evident to the more discerning layman well before the promulgation of the new Mass in 1969. Christopher Sykes, the biographer of

Evelyn Waugh, commented in an article published in 1966:

"The average Catholic layman is most aware of the *Aggiornamento* movement in the Church by the experience of going to church and attending Mass in the new liturgy. We love it; we are deeply grateful for it; we have never had it so good; so we are repeatedly told. Those who don't like it are a small unintelligent minority who would cling to anything, good or bad, just because it happened to be old. We are repeatedly told this too. We are also told by many of our clergy that we were most dissatisfied with the mass as it was; that when attending it we paid no heed to its significance but, on the contrary, regarded it as the priest's business and nothing to do with us laymen, to whom it was merely a meaningless gabble in a language we particularly disliked. We were all very happy, so we are told, to have done with the old Mass.

"The propaganda in favor of the new rite, which I have not caricatured above, strikes me as being particularly weak in respect of the alleged general dislike of Catholics for the former rite. It is weak as a propaganda point, because the same clergy told us for years, certainly since I can remember first hearing a sermon or a religious instruction, that the Mass bound us into a fellowship because (doctrine apart) love of the Mass was an emotion which we shared...(The vernacular) would weaken that majestic unity of the Church reflected in its ceremony. We were told that such a custom would offend far more people than it would please, and do far more harm than good. When the same people turn round and congratulate us on having got rid of the bad old liturgy, and promise us more vernacular and less and less of the Mass as we were said to love it, what are we to believe? Were they consciously talking nonsense all those years, or are they really sincere in their criticisms (which sometimes amount to denigrations) today? Either way, the clergy who indulge in this propaganda are weakening their authority in the minds of people who can remember."[18]

# Liturgical "Doublethink"

Unfortunately, as events have proved, it seems that most Catholics do have very poor memories — or a facility for forgetting what they find inconvenient. It is impossible not to be reminded of the principle of "doublethink" utilized by the Party in Orwell's *Nineteen Eighty-Four*. It means: "...the ability to *believe* that black is white, and more, to *know* that black is white, and to forget that one has ever believed the contrary."[19]

Those who are unable or unwilling to adapt themselves to the process of doublethink are treated as mad. "You are mentally deranged. You suffer from a defective memory. You are unable to remember real events and you persuade yourself that you remember other events which never happened. Fortunately it is curable."[20]

Those of us who have not been "cured", who still remember the Mass as it was, or (where we have the good fortune) are still able to assist at the Tridentine Mass, know that it is a grotesque travesty of the truth to compare the reform of Pope Paul VI with that of Pope St. Pius V — even that most cautious of conservatives, Douglas Woodruff, spoke out against this absurd claim. "It is quite misleading to equate the rite of St. Pius V with the rite of Pope Paul VI."[21]

Douglas Woodruff is certainly one of the most distinguished lay-scholars in the English-speaking Catholic world today, but in making this statement he is only stating what should be obvious to any Catholic blessed with a modicum of common sense and an elementary knowledge of the Mass and its history. In his Catholic Truth Society pamphlet *Liturgical Changes, the Background*, Father J.D. Crichton has the effrontery to claim that: "In spite of everything, the New Order of Mass is *not* new except in one or two minor details." Bishop G. Emmet Carter, President of the Canadian Conference of Catholic Bishops, went even further by writing in the Canadian *Catholic Register* of 1 October 1977: "Spare me also the so-called Tridentine rites (sic). There is *no* substantial difference between the rite of Pope Pius V and the rite of

Pope Paul VI. And I will debate anyone on the subject. Moreover, there is no noticeable difference at all if the celebrant chooses the first eucharistic prayer or Roman Canon." It is clear that there are clerics of all ranks who consider the laity to be devoid of education and intelligence.

There would be some logic in liberals claiming that the new Mass is better than the old Mass, and that those who can't see this are mentally deranged. But to argue that what we have now is what we had before — the same Mass with a few modifications in non-essentials — well, in the world of *Nineteen Eighty-Four* this would have been termed *doubleplusdoublethink!*

No, Father Gelineau is correct. The Roman rite as we knew it no longer exists. It has been destroyed. We have witnessed not a reform but a revolution — and a triumphant revolution. To quote the euphoric words of Archbishop Bugnini, chief architect of the revolution:

"The liturgical reform is a major conquest of the Catholic Church (*la reforma liturgica è una grande conquista della Chiesa cattolica*), and has its ecumenical dimensions (*con proiezioni ecumeniche*), since the other Churches and Christian denominations see in it not only something to be admired, but equally a sign of further progress to come (*non solo l'ammirazione, ma anche una specie di batistrada*)."[22]

As Our Lord founded only one Church, the term "Churches" is, strictly speaking, only acceptable when referring to the Catholic Church in different countries, e.g., the Churches of Spain, France, Italy. Where the term "Church" is applied to bodies not in Communion with the Roman Pontiff it must clearly refer to the different branches of the Orthodox Church; I would be extremely surprised if Archbishop Bugnini could find a single member of any Orthodox Church, priest or layman, who considered the post-conciliar liturgical reform as "something to be admired". One Russian Orthodox priest remarked to me recently that after attending a new Mass he could never possibly assist at it again, since he did not see how anyone who could celebrate the Mass in such a way could

15

possibly believe in the Real Presence. It is quite indisputable that every stage in Archbishop Bugnini's reform has taken us further away from the Orthodox and nearer to Protestantism.

It is now necessary to examine the ecumenical dimension of the New Order of Mass.

# II
# AN ECUMENICAL LITURGY

Under the prophetic title *A Common Liturgy?*, an article in *The Tablet* of 15 January, 1966, expressed pleasure at the "evidence of ecumenical advance" found in the convergence between the Anglican Series II Holy Communion Service and the Catholic Mass. Series II "adopts almost exactly the precise structure of the first part of the Mass, as it is now celebrated as a result of the Council's liturgical reforms."[23] Both Catholic and Anglican liturgies have developed a great deal since 1966. The Anglicans now have their Series III Communion Service; we have our new Mass; and the nature of their common development can best be described as an accelerating convergence. It is unlikely that the changes which have taken place in either liturgy could be termed "developments" if the stringent tests laid down in Chapter V of Newman's *The Development of Christian Doctrine* are applied. He insists that a true development must be conservative of what has gone before it and that "a developed doctrine which reverses the course of development which has preceded it is no true development but a corruption".

Where the Anglican Communion Service is concerned, the previous development had been to positively exclude the Catholic doctrine of the Mass; a doctrine which Cranmer fully understood, abhorred, and rejected — as is proved conclusively in Francis Clark's magisterial study, *Eucharistic Sacrifice and the Reformation*. In a vindication of the Bull *Apostolicae Curae*, published in 1898, the Catholic bishops explained: "To put the matter briefly, if the First Prayer Book of Edward VI is compared with the Missal, sixteen omissions can be detected, the evident purpose of which was to eliminate the idea of sacrifice. Moreover, whereas even after that drastic treatment there still remained a few phrases and rubrics on which Gardiner could fasten, endeavoring to understand them as still asserting the Real Objective Presence and the True Sacrifice, all these phrases were altered in the revised

Prayer Book of 1552."[24] As will be shown below, the Series III Service *reverses* this course of development by employing a form of words more open to a Catholic interpretation but which at the same time, in what must be something of a triumph even for Anglican comprehensiveness, is calculated to conciliate the Free Churches!

Where the new Mass is concerned, the reversal of development occurs by denuding the liturgy of prayers expressing explicitly the doctrines of the Real Objective Presence and the True Sacrifice which it had absorbed by a gradual and natural process during a period of fifteen hundred years; a process fully in accord with Newman's third characteristic of a true development, the power of assimilation. As is explained in Canon Smith's *The Teaching of the Catholic Church*, "...throughout the history of the development of the sacramental liturgy, the tendency has been towards growth — additions and accretions, the effort to obtain a fuller, more perfect symbolism."[25] This was a key point in the Catholic bishops' vindication of *Apostolicae Curae*. "That in earlier times local Churches were permitted to *add* new prayers and ceremonies is acknowledged...But that they were also permitted to subtract prayers and ceremonies in previous use, and even to remodel the existing rites in the most drastic manner, is a proposition for which we know of no historical foundation, and which appears to us absolutely incredible."[26] To understand why the Catholic Church has broken with her unvarying tradition, and remodeled the Roman rite in the most drastic manner, it is necessary to begin with Vatican II.

On the Feast of the Annunciation, 1963, Archbishop Marcel Lefebvre sent a letter assessing the first session of the Second Vatican Council to all the members of the Congregation of the Holy Ghost of which he was Superior-General. The Archbishop had noted a number of disturbing tendencies among the Council Fathers, including that of an important group which placed the ecumenical aspect of the Council before all else. This group wished to purge the conciliar texts of anything which might tend to keep alive differences rather than assist in bringing about unity.[27]

✓ Protestant observers at the Council did far more than observe; some, such as Oscar Cullmann, a Lutheran, actually made what was described in the *Osservatore Romano* as "a valid contribution" to the drawing up of conciliar texts.[28]

✓ I have already provided ample documentation of the manner in which the Protestant observers influenced the conciliar texts (see *Pope John's Council*, Chapter IX), and will not repeat it here. It will suffice to add a testimony which I did not include by Archdeacon Pawley, and Anglican observer.

"In the course of the Council itself the fullest courtesies and opportunities for communication and exchange were allowed to the observers at every stage, and traces of the process can be recognized in the documents themselves."[29]

Another of the Anglican observers, Bishop Moorman, of Ripon, remarked that:

"In reading the Schema on the Liturgy, and in listening to the debate on it, I could not help thinking that, if the Church of Rome went on improving the Missal an Breviary long enough, they would one day invent the Book of Common Prayer."[30]

Another Protestant theologian, Dr. Jaroslav Pelikan, gave a qualified but enthusiastic welcome to the Constitution on the Liturgy which, he explains: "...does not merely tinker with the formalities of liturgical worship, but seeks to form and to reform the very life of the Church. Since that was also the very aim of the Reformers of the 16th century, it will perhaps be appropriate for me, as a Reformation scholar, to summarize my reactions to the Constitution under three of the rubrics I employed in my book *Obedient Rebels* (Harper, 1964) for an interpretation of the liturgical thought of Martin Luther." Dr. Pelikan could have gone on to point out that the aim of the Protestant Reformers in the changes they made in the liturgy was, as explained by Luther, to destroy the Mass and, in so doing, destroy the Church, *"Tolle Missam, tolle ecclesiam"*. However, Dr. Pelikan evidently judged it prudent to pass over this point. He does explain that several of the fundamental principles of the *Constitution on the Liturgy* "represent the acceptance, however belated, of the liturgical program set forth by the Reformers..."

Dr. Pelikan's enthusiasm is not unqualified, however. Commenting on statements in the *Liturgy Constitution*, which accorded with Protestant thinking, he adds: "Such statements are bound to evoke the enthusiastic approval of anyone who believes that the Reformation was the work of the Holy Spirit, but this reaction is turned to disappointment at one crucial point. In view of the explicit commandment of Christ and the evident practice of the early Church, what is the justification for still denying the chalice to the laity except at a very few special occasions — 'in cases to be determined by the Apostolic See' (Article 55 of the *Constitution*)? At the very least, the restoration of the form of communion prescribed by Our Lord must be a primary task for the reform of the liturgy in the near future."[31]

There is, of course, no theological objection to the reception of Holy Communion under both kinds — nor is there any theological objection to reception under one kind, although Protestants maintain that there is. Reception under both kinds was one of the key issues in the liturgical disputes of the Reformation and its acceptance as the normal practice could appear to concede that reception under one kind, the almost invariable practice in the Western Church since the 14th century, was objectionable in some way, and would, as Cardinal Godfrey of Westminster pointed out during the debate on the *Liturgy Constitution*, "lead people to think that the Catholic Church was giving in to the Anglicans and some of the other Protestant bodies who had retained this practice."[32]

However, Dr. Pelikan's demand for the Catholic Church to restore "the form of communion prescribed by Our Lord" is being steadily implemented. Fr. Schillebeeckx, the extreme liberal Dutch *peritus* (expert) at the Council, has revealed how some *periti* had admitted introducing ambiguous phrases into the conciliar texts which they intended to exploit after the Council through the commissions set up to implement the official documents.[33]

The short phrase quoted by Dr. Pelikan from Article 55 of the *Constitution on the Liturgy* regarding the introduction of Communion under both kinds "in cases to be determined by the Holy See" was soon expanded into a very lengthy list in the *Institutio Generalis* to the new Mass.[34] This list has since been expanded again, and in some parishes optional Communion under both kinds is now a regular practice. This, of course, is unofficial, but if events follow what has become the established practice, the Vatican will eventually bring an end to this defiance of the law by permitting it, as has happened with Communion in the hand and the distribution of Holy Communion by laymen.

In a similar manner, such Protestant practices as the vernacular liturgy have become virtually universal, despite the fact that the Council ordered the retention of Latin and the majority of the Fathers were under the impression that it would certainly be retained "in the principle parts of the Mass in those countries where the Church was long established and the people were used to it, reserving the vernacular for the catechetical or dialogue portion at the beginning of the Mass, and for all other liturgical functions".[35] Cardinal Heenan has admitted that "the bishops at the Council failed to foresee that Latin would virtually disappear from Catholic churches."[36]

Similarly, the introduction of Mass facing the people, a step in full harmony with "the liturgical programs" set forth by the (Protestant) Reformers, has become virtually universal in the Western Church outside the Iron Curtain. This break with the liturgical tradition of both Catholic and Orthodox Churches was, like the widespread practice of Communion in the hand, not even mentioned in the *Liturgy Constitution*. Communion in the hand is also contrary to the traditions of the Eastern Churches, both Orthodox and Uniat, and it is certain that the closer we align ourselves with Protestant belief and practice, the more we alienate ourselves from the Orthodox.[37]

Before even beginning to deal with changes in the text of the Mass designed to bring it into line with Protestant Eucharistic practice and belief, it is evident that the changes already mentioned — the universal use of the vernacular, Mass facing the people, and Communion in the hand — would in themselves have served to transform the ethos of even the old Mass from what had been regarded as, and was recognized as, a *Catholic* ethos, to one that was most certainly Protestant.

The implementation of the *Liturgy Constitution* was entrusted to a *Consilium* which included six Protestant advisers. Archbishop Dwyer, formerly of Portland, Oregon, has conceded that the great mistake of the Council Fathers was to let the reform of the liturgy get into the hands of these members of the "liturgical establishment".[38] *La Documentation Catholique* of 3 May, 1970, carried a picture of Pope Paul with the six Protestant advisers, when he received the members of the *Consilium* for the last time on 10 April 1970, its work having been completed. Jean Madiran, editor of *Itinéraires*, made a particularly perceptive comment regarding the photograph and the accompanying report, in his issue of December 1973.

"The *Novus Ordo Missae* was," he wrote, "the achievement par excellence, the masterpiece of this *Consilium* which had created it with the active co-operation of six heretics, the six who can be seen in the photograph to the right of the Holy Father.

'I use the term 'heretics' without the least intention of being aggressive, offensive, or even rhetorical. I use it because it is the correct scientific term, the exact term. Not only are these six heretical individuals heretics personally, but they are there in their official capacity as such. *La Documentation Catholique* makes this clear in note 1 to page 416. It names the six as Dr. George, Canon Jasper, Dr. Shepherd, Dr. Kunneth, Dr. Smith, and Brother Max Thurian, and affirms that they are there as 'representing respectively the World Council of Churches, the Anglican and Lutheran communions, and the Taize community'. The *Novus Ordo Missae* was not simply concocted in collaboration and in agreement with six people possessing expert knowledge, individually chosen for their international reputation or their good looks and who, by chance as it were, also happened to be heretics. No. The *Novus Ordo Missae* was concocted in connivance with six official representatives of a number of heresies and convoked specifically in this capacity to organize our liturgical renewal. They produced exactly the type of liturgy and the type of renewal that could have been expected, in view of what they represented."

On page 417 of the same edition of *La Documentation Catholique,* Pope Paul is reported as expressing thanks to the members of the *Consilium* for the manner in which they had "...re-edited in a new manner liturgical texts tried and tested by long usage or established formulas which were *completely new*." He went on to thank them for "imparting greater theological value to the liturgical texts so that the *lex orandi* conformed better with the *lex credendi*".

## Lex orandi, lex credendi

An accepted principle in regard to liturgical worship is that the doctrinal standpoint of a Christian body must necessarily be reflected in its worship. Liturgical rites should express what they contain. It is not necessary for the Catholic position to be expressly contradicted for a rite to become suspect; the suppression of prayers which had given liturgical expression to the doctrine behind the rite is more than sufficient to give cause for concern. This principle is embodied in the phrase *"legem credendi lex statuat supplicandi"* (let the law of prayer fix the law of faith) — in other words, the liturgy of the Church is a sure guide to her teaching. This is usually presented in the abbreviated form of *lex orandi, lex credendi,* and can be translated freely as meaning that the manner in which the Church worships *(lex orandi)* must reflect what the Church believes *(lex credendi).* It would be a mistake to expect to be able to deduce a system of doctrine from the liturgical books of any Christian body and to attempt to do this would be a misuse of the principle under discussion here. A study of the liturgy is perhaps most useful as a background to doctrinal belief — but where changes, particularly omissions, are made, the doctrine behind the revised liturgy becomes very much clearer.

Jean Madiran considers that Pope Paul's statement concerning the greater theological value of the new texts is of capital importance. He notes that it evidently means that until 1969 the liturgical texts did not possess the degree of theological value which was desirable! He writes:

"...they did not have that theological value which is now to be found in the 'completely new' formulas of the new liturgies. It's a point of view. For more than a thousand years the *lex orandi* of the Church had not been sufficiently in accord with the *lex credendi*. The new Eucharistic prayers conform better than the Roman Canon with the true faith; this is also the opinion of the Taizé community, the Anglican and Lutheran communions, and of the World Council of Churches..."

The *Novus Ordo Missae* was described in Article 7 of its original *Institutio Generalis* as: "The Lord's Supper, or the Mass, is the sacred assembly or gathering together of the people of God, with a priest presiding, to celebrate the memorial of the Lord. For this reason, the promise of Christ is particularly true of a local congregation of the Church: where two or three are gathered together in my name, there am I in their midst." This is a wholly Protestant concept and has been replaced in the revised *Institutio Generalis* with one which, if not totally satisfactory, is at least recognizably Catholic. It should be noted that even in the original *Institutio Generalis* there was a reference to the eucharistic sacrifice of Christ's Body and Blood in Article 2, but it was Article 7 which provided the basis for the instruction on the new Mass and most perfectly expressed its ethos. Father Bryan Houghton remembers the well-known lecture on the new Mass which was delivered in various parts of the country by Father J.D. Crichton, one of the two most enthusiastic advocates of the new liturgy in England, the other being Father Clifford Howell, S.J. Father Houghton remarked that the

The Tridentine Mass at the altar of Our Lady of the Fields, of the Society of Saint Pius X's Seminary, Ecône, Switzerland (celebrated by Archbishop Marcel Lefebvre).

lecture "revolved principally around clause 7 of the General Instruction: 'The Mass is the synaxis or congregation of the people of God...' This, we were told, was the basic text on which priests would be formed in our seminaries for generations to come. It was, of course, repealed and rewritten within six months...However, Fr. Crichton was not invited back to give an amended version of his well-known lecture...We all then traipsed into the Church of the English Martyrs to watch Fr. Crichton perform...with the dignity of which short, round men alone are capable. The gloom was absolute."[39]

In my forthcoming book *Pope Paul's New Mass* I will document the conformity of the *lex orandi* of the *Novus Ordo Missae* with the *lex credendi* of the original Article 7 — a rite and definition which Protestants themselves have praised as being compatible with, or very close to, their own concept of the Lord's Supper. As Cardinals Ottaviani and Bacci insisted, in their letter to Pope Paul, the new Mass "represents, as whole and in detail, a striking departure from the Catholic theology of the Holy Mass as it was formulated in Session XXII of the Council of Trent, which, by fixing definitely the 'canons' of the rite, erected an insurmountable barrier against any heresy which might attack the integrity of the Mystery."[40] It cannot be sufficiently emphasized that this is the considered judgment of two Cardinals distinguished both by their theological competence and their devotion to the Holy See.[*]

The only effective means of overcoming an insurmountable barrier is to remove it — and this is exactly what the *Consilium* did to the Mass of St. Pius V.

The extent to which the new Mass departs from the theology of the Council of Trent can best be gauged by comparing the prayers which the *Consilium* removed from the liturgy with those removed by Cranmer. The coincidence is not simply striking — it is horrifying. It cannot,

---

[*]   It has been falsely alleged that Cardinal Ottaviani withdrew his criticism. This allegation is conclusively refuted in *The New Mass*, pp. 22-26 (Augustine Pamphlets No. 3)

in fact, be a coincidence. The *Judica me, Confiteor,* Offertory Prayers, *Placeat Tibi,* Last Gospel — these are just a few — and it was by omissions rather than by the inclusion of specifically heretical prayers that the Protestant Reformers achieved their aims. It was, above all, through the liturgy, the *lex orandi,* that the *lex credendi* (in those countries where the Reformers gained the support of the temporal power) was transformed from the Catholic to a Protestant norm. The *lex credendi,* which the *lex orandi* of the new Mass manifests, is perhaps best illustrated by the replacement of the *Suscipe Sancte Pater* in the old Offertory by a prayer referring to bread "which earth has given and human hands have made".[41]

In discussing the changes in the Mass, mention must be made of another similarity between this reform and that of Cranmer. In his first (1549) Prayer Book, Cranmer was careful to ensure that the rite he provided could still be interpreted in a Catholic sense. Had he insisted upon a rite which could not possibly be seen as anything but Protestant, he might have been faced with an open revolt by a large section of the clergy. In the initial stages of his reform he made it possible for conservative priests to convince themselves that what they were now celebrating was still a Mass. The *Novus Ordo Missae* has done the same by the provision of alternatives. A truncated *Confiteor* can be used — but alternative penitential rites are available containing nothing to which a Protestant could object. The Roman Canon *can* still be used — but it need not be. It is thus possible to celebrate a Mass in one church, particularly where Latin is used, which will appear to differ very little from the old one, whereas in the parish next door the form could differ very little from that used in many Anglican churches, and this without any deviations from the official text approved by the Pope.

Attempts have been made to minimize the role played by the six Protestant observers and stress has been laid upon the fact that they were not allowed to vote at the Plenary Sessions.[42] In the Council itself, as Bishop Lucey of Cork and Ross has pointed out, the "experts" who worked behind the scenes drafting the Council documents, were the people with real power and were more influential than most bishops.[43] In a similar manner, in the case of the *Norvus Ordo Missae,* the work of the *Consilium* was accomplished principally in the preparatory phases which led up to the Plenary Sessions. The Protestant observers were able not only to use their influence during preparatory work, but were allowed to attend the Plenary Sessions and, on at least one occasion, were actually permitted to speak during a Plenary Session — a revelation which, had it not been made by the Secretary of the Liturgical Commission of England and Wales, would almost defy belief.[44]

While on the subject of Father Boylan, whose evidence has been quoted in Note 42, it is far from irrelevant to cite his own explanation of the Mass which he included in a letter written to the *Catholic Herald* in his capacity as General Secretary of the Liturgical Commission.

"We come together as a Christian community, in obedience to the Founder of our community, in order to remember him and all that he did and said. We celebrate his memory and the salvation that He won for us in the way that Christians have done for nearly 2000 years: by listening to the Word of God, by responding to that word in spiritual song and prayer.

"Most important of all, we celebrate his memory in the way he himself told us to do: in the Breaking of Bread. Hopefully, we leave the celebration confirmed in our Faith and even more determined to bring to others the good news of the event that we celebrate."[45]

It does not require a prolonged study of this explanation to note that it is straightforward "Article 7" and does not contain one word which an evangelical Protestant could not accept. This is also the explanation of the Mass given in Catholic schools where teachers have been indoctrinated with the new catechetics.

But to return to the subject of the Protestant observers. The fact that they played an active part in compiling the new rite of Mass (and ordination) has been denied not simply by Fr. Boylan, who is Secretary of the Liturgical Commission of England and Wales, but by Fr. J.D. Crichton and Archbishop Bugnini among others. I have provided sufficient documentation to settle the matter once and for all in the appendix to this pamphlet.

## Towards a Common Liturgy

Facts have now emerged which provide an even more disquieting aspect to the unprecedented phenomenon of Protestants being asked to help compile a new Catholic Mass. There is evidence of a concerted scheme for different denominations to reform their respective liturgies in the direction of an eventual united Christian rite. This becomes clear simply by examining the text of the new Anglican Series III Communion Service. Material not found in the Roman Mass or the Anglican Prayer Book has suddenly found its way into the revised rites of both communions. The celebrant is referred to as the President, there are Bidding prayers and a "sign of peace"; after the Consecration the congregation says "Christ has died, Christ has risen, Christ will come again". After the Our Father, the following appears: "For the kingdom, the power, and the glory are yours now and forever". No rational person could brush this evidence aside as mere coincidence, particularly in view of the fact that an Anglican observer on the *Consilium*, Dr. Jasper, played a leading part in the compilation of the Series III service. It is hardly surprising that another Anglican minister was able to write to the London *Catholic Herald*, stating: "Today's liturgical study has brought our respective liturgies to a remarkable similarity, so that there is very little difference in the sacrificial phrasing of the prayer of oblation in the Series Three and that of Eucharistic Prayer II in the *Missa Normativa*."[46]

The Anglican Bishop of Southwark has stated on several occasions that he greatly admires the *Novus Ordo Missae*, uses it himself, and would like to see it generally available to Anglicans at least as an alternative. He has also "con-celebrated" Mass with Catholic priests when travelling on the continent![47]

M.G. Siegvalt, a professor of dogmatic theology in the Protestant faculty at Strasbourg, testifies that: "...nothing in the renewed Mass need really trouble the evangelical Protestant".[48]

Jean Guitton, a close friend of Pope Paul and a lay observer at Vatican II, quoted a Protestant journal as praising the manner in which the new Eucharistic prayers had dropped "the false perspective of a sacrifice offered to God".[49]

A Swedish Lutheran praised the reform because it had taken: "A notable step forward in the ecumenical field and has drawn near the liturgical forms of the Lutheran Church."[50]

From the opposite standpoint, Fr. H.O. Waterhouse, S.J., finds much to enthuse over in the Anglican Series III Communion Service.

"I attended the service and was immensely struck by the similarity of the service chosen (Series 3) to the Mass as we now have it in the West. The words, the actions and the very structure of the service seem to be a replica of that to which we are now getting accustomed ourselves in the Catholic Church. If Series III comes to be widely used by Anglicans it will surely provide a good preparation for the day when intercommunion becomes possible."[51]

Writing in the February 1974 issue of *Veritas*, journal of the Anglican Association, the editor, Canon C.B. Armstrong, points out that Series III is intended not only to approximate to the *Novus Ordo Missae* but to be acceptable to Protestants of a far more Evangelical nature than the Church of England. "In form it approximates closely to the new Roman Mass, omitting a few doctrinal statements which would not be likely to find general acceptance in England. In matter it avoids being specific, as will be seen, on doctrines which would not be accepted by nonconformists...its main objects seem to be (1) to keep outwardly in line with the liturgical reforms on the Continent, and (2) to conciliate the Free Churches of this country and overseas with the hope of producing a United Christian rite in a United Christian Church."

Canon Armstrong was writing from an Anglo-Catholic standpoint, but Evangelical Anglicans have also noted the ambiguous nature of the new services being foisted upon them. An editorial in the *English Churchman,* an Evangelical Anglican journal, sounded a warning of commendable honesty that the new Anglican services had a Rome-ward slant. This is quite correct in the sense that the Series III service can be celebrated in a manner that has a Catholic slant, in other words, the new Anglican services are open to a Catholic interpretation without, however, specifically affirming any Catholic teaching. The editorial reads:

"We have, since the beginning of liturgical experiment, been trying to point out that the new services are taking the Church of England in a Rome-ward direction. They are not merely new services linguistically, but have a definite doctrinal and liturgical orientation. In fact, they are not new services at all, but merely revamped versions of the 1549 service which, as any student of church history knows, was a half-way house between the medieval mass and the Communion service based upon Scriptural doctrines.

"The unsatisfactory nature of the 1549 Book became clear to the Reformers, who realized that they must move on to a truly reformed service, which is substantially that of the 1662 Book.

"The similarities between the services of Series II and III Holy Communion and the Roman mass in the vernacular are apparent not only to the doctrinally informed, but even to the uninitiated who may happen to be present at these services. It is seen in the overall rearrangement of the parts of the service, and also in the subtle alteration of words here and there, which change its emphasis and direction. But, of course, *Series II and III are not yet the same as the Roman mass. They are a half-way house, a sort of liturgical hybrid, deliberately constructed for the purpose of bridging the gap between a reformed Church of England and the unreformed Church of Rome.* Nobody can deny the success they have had in doing this, particularly amongst Evangelical churchmen. But the same logic and constraints apply to these services as applied to the half-reformed service of 1549. They cannot remain indefinitely where they are. They must eventually move further in one direction or another. There are only two coherent doctrinal and liturgical positions; either that of the Reformation and Scripture, or that of Roman dogma and tradition. It must be abundantly clear in which direction the architects of change in the Church of England desire to take the new services eventually."[52]

Further evidence of such a convergence has been provided by Rev. D. Stacey, a member of the National Faith and Order Committee which produced the new Methodist communion service. Writing in the August 1969 issue of the *Catholic Gazette* he explains that this "new rite is an ecumenical service. It goes without saying that we have studied everything that others have done before us and borrowed ideas though only very rarely actual words, from other rites. This is a good time to be revising. There is widespread interest and experiment. As soon as a substantial draft of the new service had been prepared it was sent all over the world to liturgical scholars of every ecclesiastical allegiance including, naturally, Roman Catholics. The comments generally were tremendously valuable. In the liturgical field, names and sects and parties are falling and, though one must not exaggerate, it is possible now to dream of a form of Eucharist to which all Christians might eventually subscribe."

An almost identical assessment of the current situation also appeared in 1969, in the February issue of *Concilium* — and ultra "progressive" journal founded and largely edited by liberal *periti* (experts) at Vatican II. In an article entitled *W.C.C. and Liturgical Reform*, details are given of a group formed under the auspices of the World Council of Churches entitled the *Societas Liturgica*. It includes Anglican, Baptist, Lutheran, Catholic, Methodist, and Orthodox "liturgiologists", more than half of whom are members of "national or confessional liturgical commissions". The report concludes that: "There is a growing consensus about the nature of Christian worship. This growing agreement gradually finds expression in words and rites, in atmosphere and every kind of liturgical activity. For some the process is too gradual but the progress of this converging and understanding of the faith is in any case most promising."[53]

Another body formed to promote liturgical convergence is the ICET, the International Consultation on English Texts. It is an interdenominational body and its members belong to most of the English-speaking Christian Churches. "Its brief", according to the Autumn 1974 issue of *Music and Liturgy*, "is to propose texts which will be acceptable to all the Churches who are represented on it, in the hope of furthering ecumenism." The Catholic bishops of England and Wales made a number of the ICET texts mandatory in 1975, thus bringing the new Mass even more into line with the Series III Communion Service which already incorporates these texts. Our bishops have not yet accepted all the ICET texts and *Music and Liturgy* takes them to task for their "half-hearted attempt to meet the demands of ecumenism. It appears that the bishops' hands have been forced even this far by a *fait accompli* — which is to say that many people all over Great Britain have been using ICET texts for some time."

The reason for our bishops' lack of enthusiasm was made apparent to everyone when the ICET texts were made mandatory in March 1975. It is interesting to note that the Catholic Truth Society had already incorporated these texts into the 1974 edition of its *Simple Prayer Book*, published well before the end of the year; making it clear that the imposition of these texts was very much a question of a *fait accompli*. One archbishop issued an *ad clerum* explaining that while he personally regretted the changes, the Holy See is anxious to have a common version for English-speaking countries and that we have decided to go along with the others. He did not specify exactly where the others are going! It is unlikely that the tolerance shown to priests who have been using the ICET texts in defiance of the bishops will be extended to any priests declining to use them when they are imposed. The commentator in *Music and Liturgy* seems confident that the ICET texts which the bishops have failed to adopt, such as the *Agnus Dei* and *Our Father*, will eventually be imposed upon the faithful by a continuing use of the *fait accompli* technique, but regrets that this will have to happen "in the course of the next few years, due to a process of *force mejeure* by the people (including priests, liturgists, musicians, etc.), in dribs and drabs instead of at one fell swoop now that the door has at least been partially opened".

It is clear that given the convergence between the new Mass and the Anglican Series III, and the compatibility of Series III with nonconformist belief, the new Mass must now be acceptable to Protestants well to the theological left of the Church of England. Evidence in this respect is not lacking. Max Thurian, a member of the Protestant monastic community of Taizé, in France, and another of the six observers, is reported in *La Croix* (May 30, 1969) as stating that the *Norvus Ordo Missae* now makes it possible for non-Catholics to celebrate the Lord's Supper with the same prayers as Catholics. Since then, the Superior Consistory of the ultra-Protestant Church of the Confession of Augsburg of Alsace-Lorraine issued a statement after its meeting in Strasburg on 8 December 1973, in which it approves the reception of Holy Communion by its members in Catholic churches. (The Catholic Bishop of Strasburg, in defiance of even the present liberal legislation, permits intercommunion and concelebration with Protestants.) The Statement reads: "We consider that in the present circumstances fidelity to the Gospel and to our tradition does not allow us to forbid the members of our Church to participate in a Catholic Eucharistic celebration.

"However, we must act with great discernment and wisdom: the invitation of another Church should not be accepted unless we can personally recognize in its Eucharistic practice the celebration of the Supper such as the Lord instituted it. Given the present form of Eucharistic celebration in the Catholic Church, and by reason of the present convergence in theology, many obstacles which might have prevented a Protestant from participating in its Eucharistic celebration seem to be on the way to disappearing. It should be possible for a Protestant today to recognize in the Catholic Eucharistic celebration the Supper instituted by the Lord.

"In particular it behoves us to watch the following points: The evangelical character of the celebration in which a Protestant could participate must be evident. We particularly insist upon communion under both kinds, not only in fidelity to the Gospel and to the Reformation, but because this practice, for us, is opposed to a certain appearance of clericalism. We attach great importance to the use of the new prayers with which we feel at home, and which have the advantage of giving a different interpretation to the theology of sacrifice than we were accustomed to attribute to Catholicism. These prayers invite us to recognize an evangelical theology of sacrifice."[54]

Among the points which it is worth underlining here is the fact that not only do these Protestants feel at home with the prayers of the new Mass, but they state explicitly that they consider that there has been a change in the Catholic theology of the Mass which brings it into line with evangelical teaching on the Lord's Supper. It is also interesting to note the introduction of Communion under both kinds being interpreted in precisely the manner foreseen by Cardinal Godfrey (see page 20).

This change in the theology of the Mass as expressed in the *Novus Ordo Missae* has also been remarked upon by the Anglican theologian, Dr. J.W. Charley, who has played a prominent part in preparing the two Agreed Statements — on the Eucharist and the Ministry — issued by the Anglican-Roman Catholic International Commission. On page 17 of his commentary on the *Windsor Agreement on the Eucharist*, Dr. Charley states:

"Much of what Küng has called 'the valid demands of the Reformers' has now been met by the Church of Rome in the new Eucharistic Prayers, even though in these there remain echoes of the pre-Reformation language of Eucharistic Sacrifice..."

In his Commentary on the *Canterbury Agreement*, on the Ministry, he explains:

"Faced with this range of agreed material, one is compelled to ask one searching question: Is there not here a change of theological stance on the part of Roman Catholicism? If 'change' is too strong a word, then at least there seems to be a considerable shift of emphasis when these documents are compared with previous official statements. If one can detect a new trend, how far is it likely to go?"

In this second quotation Dr. Charley is referring to the texts of the Agreed Statements, but there can be no doubt that no Agreements could have been reached professing to show that Catholics and Anglicans share the same belief in the Eucharist and the priesthood had the old Mass, with such prayers as the *Suscipe Sancte Pater*, or the *Placeat Tibi*, still been in universal use in the Roman rite. Study them and decide for yourself. The obvious correspondence between the convergence in the *lex orandi* of Catholic and Anglican worship, and the *lex credendi* of the Agreed Statements, was brought out clearly by the Venerable Bernard Pawley, Archdeacon of Canterbury, as reported in the *Catholic Herald* of 18 October 1974. Commenting on the unanimous welcome given by the Convocations of Canterbury and York to the Agreed Statement on Ministry and Ordination, the report quotes Archdeacon Pawley as pronouncing it a "remarkable development" bolstered by an "unbelievable convergence" in the liturgical practice of the two churches. "It is little short of a miracle that in so short a time we have come so far," said the Archdeacon (an Anglican observer at Vatican II). "Without a doubt it represents the hand of God on the Church in our generation." So far have we come, in fact, that Catholics and Anglicans are now building joint churches and sharing joint tabernacles in Britain.

---

\*    In a letter published in *The Universe* of 30 January 1976, David Catling, chairman of the Cippenham Shared Church Trust, stated that: "the insistent and unanimous request of the Board and with the express permission of the two diocesan bishops, the Anglican and Catholic reservation are housed in the one tabernacle, albeit separately."

What, it seems permissible to wonder, would the Catholic martyrs who died rather than deny that the Blessed Sacrament is God, and the Protestant martyrs who died rather than affirm it, think about all this?

"All these changes have but one justification," commented Archbishop Lefebvre in the May 1974 issue of *World Trends*, "an aberrant senseless ecumenism that will not attract a single Protestant to the Faith but will cause countless Catholics to lose it, and will instill total confusion in the minds of many more who will no longer know what is true and what is false?" The point has now been reached where High Church Anglican services appear more Catholic than those taking place in most Catholic churches. In a visit to the U.S.A. in 1972, Dr. Ramsey, Anglican Archbishop of Canterbury, remarked: "I have experienced Roman rites which are really very Anglican. If you want to find rites that are really Roman, visit some of our old-fashioned Anglo-Catholic shrines."[55]

## The Case for the New Mass

There are, as Dr. Charley observed, still some "echoes of the pre-Reformation language of Eucharistic Sacrifice" in the new Mass, even when celebrated with Canon II. There is the prayer that the gifts "may *become* for us the body and blood of our Lord Jesus Christ". Series III asks that the gifts "may *be* to us his body and blood". "Become" implies the notion of a real change more strongly than "be" — although the addition of "for us" does facilitate an interpretation in line with the theory of transignification, where the Presence of Christ in the Sacrament is really only for the believer and not in the order of objective reality. Transignification is a doctrine fully in line with that of the Protestant Reformers. Hugh Ross Williamson has pointed out that the inclusion of "for us" (*nobis*) in the Roman Canon cannot be interpreted in this equivocal sense, "for the transubstantiation has been prepared for by the magnificent *Te Igitur, Memento Domine,* and *Hanc Igitur,* where the 'holy and unblemished sacrificial gifts' are described in terms proper to the coming change into the Body and Blood, of which we are the unworthy beneficiaries".[56] He considers that the use of the new formula in Canon II "makes it possible for any of the member sects of the World Council of Churches to use it as their communion service".[57]

A point which it would be hard to interpret in a Protestant manner is the rubric instructing the priest to kneel and adore after the Consecration. This, however, is only a rubric and does not hinder the emergence of a "united Christian rite" as regards at least the invariable parts of the text. This is also the case with the Secret Prayers, many of which are extremely sacrificial in tone but could be omitted by any sect not wishing to use them. These prayers have been considerably modified in the ICET translations.

It is also true that all the new Eucharistic Prayers include a specific offering of the Body and Blood of Christ after the Consecration. This is in sharp contrast with all the liturgies of Protestant denominations (including the Series III Communion Service) in which every formula which could even remotely be construed as constituting a sacrificial offering has been excluded. In Eucharistic Prayer III, in particular, the formula is most specific — a Lutheran commentator has described it as "scarcely tolerable".[58]

The weakest formula is in Eucharistic Prayer II — "We offer you the bread of life and the cup of salvation (sic)." It could hardly be more muted. But weak as it is, this formula alone suffices to make even Canon II unacceptable to the more discerning Protestants who insist in upholding the axioms upon which their theology is based. But others find that they can reconcile it with their own belief. One Lutheran pastor, in an article full of praise for the new Mass, writes:

"Thus in my Hamburg parish, for instance, we regularly use Eucharistic Prayer II, with the Lutheran form of the words of institution and omitting the prayer for the Pope."[59]

It is also interesting to note that Protestant ecumenists are devising an interpretation which will permit the acceptance of sacrificial phrasing in the Mass. I explained in *Cranmer's Godly Order* that the Reformers taught that we all have a duty to offer sacrifice, one of lauds, thanksgiving and ourselves. As Christ is present in the congregation, and as we offer ourselves, some Protestants consider that it is permissible to say that Christ is offered in the Eucharist.[60] The bread and wine can be considered as signifying the congregation which has offered them.

It is worthy of particular note that, unlike the Roman Canon, and Eucharistic Prayers III and IV, Eucharistic Prayer Number II does not contain the word *Hostia* (victim).

Some of the orthodox defenders of the new Mass might answer that the fact that the word *Hostia* occurs in two of the first three new Eucharistic Prayers to be introduced is a point in favor of the new Mass. On the contrary, if the aim was to provide a form of Mass acceptable to Protestants and only one new Eucharistic Prayer, designed to do this, had been introduced, the intention would have been blatantly obvious. By bringing in three new Prayers attention was diverted from Canon II. It must also be noted that in *not one* of the new Eucharistic Prayers is it made clear that the Consecration is effected by the priest alone, and that he is not acting as spokesman or president of a concelebrating congregation. For a Protestant, the minister possesses no powers denied to a layman. Ordination is simply a public ceremony denoting that the congregation has authorized him to exercise an office, one of his duties being to preside at the celebration of the Eucharist.

Many readers will be shocked to learn that the American hierarchy is actually preparing the way for Catholic acceptance of the concept that the sacrifice in the Mass is that of Christ being offered in virtue of His presence in the congregation who offer themselves. In the official *Newsletter* of the Bishops' Committee on the Liturgy, a ruling was laid down that when distributing Holy Communion a priest *must not* say: "Receive the Body of Christ" or "This is the Body of Christ." The reason given is that the congregation itself is the Body of Christ.

"The use of the phrase *The Body of Christ: Amen*, in the communion rite asserts in a very forceful way the presence and role of the community. The minister (sic) acknowledges who the person is by reason of baptism and confirmation and what the community is and does in the liturgical action...The change to the use of the phrase *The Body of Christ* rather than the long formula which was previously said by the priest has several repercussions in the liturgical renewal. First, it seeks to highlight the important concept, of the community as the Body of Christ; secondly it brings into focus the assent of the individual in the worshipping community, and finally it demonstrates the importance of Christ's presence in liturgical celebrations as evinced in the Constitution on the Liturgy (See no 7)."[61]

Finally, on the subject of prayers which are not compatible with Protestantism, there is the *Ecce Agnus Dei* before Holy Communion. "This *is* the lamb of God" is a very positive affirmation of the Real Presence.

Other prayers which have been cited as incompatible with Protestantism are not really so. The *Orate Fratres* can easily be interpreted as referring to a sacrifice of praise when used in a rite denuded of references to the true sacrifice of the Mass. The reference to Our Lady and the Saints in Canon II is phrased in a manner acceptable even to evangelical Protestants, and is, in any case, paralleled in Cranmer's 1549 Communion Service. It is also important to note that, on 27 April 1973, the Sacred Congregation for Divine Worship authorized the composition of still more Eucharistic Prayers and it would be surprising if some do not appear containing not even the least echo of any "pre-Reformation language of Eucharistic sacrifice". Just as Cranmer's 1549 Mass was simply an interim measure designed to pave the way for further changes, so the *Novus Ordo Missae* has been subject to continual modifications which bring it ever closer to the norms laid down by the Protestant Reformers.

Just how close it has now come was made clear by Dr. Charley in a lecture delivered at London Colney, Herts, on 11 November 1974. He spoke enthusiastically of a Mass which he had attended containing virtually nothing with which he, as an evangelical, could disagree but for one phrase in the Thanksgiving Prayer (Canon). He knew, however, that many of his Roman Catholic colleagues did not mean by it what they actually say — "they may say it but they don't actually mean it, so they assure me." He went on to add that anyone who did a little research would find that the common ground between Series III and the new Mass is the liturgy of the Church of South India — though neither Church seemed keen to admit this! (The Church of South India was formed by uniting Anglicans and Free Churches into one body. It resulted in a good number of Anglican clergymen becoming Catholics as they correctly interpreted this step as incompatible with Anglican claims to apostolic orders — Hugh Ross Williamson is the most notable of these converts.)

# III
# A QUALIFICATION

Sufficient evidence should have been provided in this pamphlet to prove that there are definite parallels between the reform of Archbishop Bugnini and the reform of Cranmer and other Protestant heresiarchs. I have been astonished to find some priests asserting in public that no "parallel" exists. What they are doing is confusing the word "parallel" with the word "identity". I have nowhere alleged that there is complete identity between the reforms of Archbishop Bugnini and Cranmer. The fact that the present reform has been approved by the Pope and permits the use of the Roman Canon is sufficient to disprove any allegation of complete identity. (The few minor changes in the Roman Canon, while totally deplorable, do not make it in the least compatible with Protestant doctrine.)

On the other hand, the introduction of the vernacular, the abolition of most of the Offertory prayers, the replacement of altars by tables, Communion in the hand, and Communion under both kinds, all constitute obvious parallels which no honest person could overlook. These are only a few — I shall provide a complete list in *Pope Paul's New Mass*. Meanwhile, readers who are interested would find it a fruitful exercise to examine Cranmer's innovations, as set out in Chapter 12 of *Cranmer's Godly Order*, and compare them with the innovations imposed by Archbishop Bugnini, the supreme architect of the post-conciliar reform.

I would also not wish to give the impression that the buffoonery castigated by Fr. Bouyer (see p. 7) is by any means universal, particularly in the British Isles. In Britain at least, my impression is that most of the clergy celebrate the new Mass with as much dignity as possible. Indeed, where it is sung in Latin facing the altar, as in the Brompton Oratory, many Catholics would imagine that they were taking part in a Tridentine Mass. This, however, is no new phenomenon. Luther was able to boast:

"Thank God...our churches are so arranged that a layman, an Italian say, or a Spaniard, who cannot understand our preaching, seeing our Mass, choir, organs, bells, etc., would surely say...there is no difference between it and his own."[62]

It goes without saying that no traditionalist should ever attribute unworthy motives to any priest who is known to be orthodox but continues to use the new rite. It must be remembered that many orthodox priests (and laypeople) find it scandalous that any Catholic can refuse to conform with directives approved by the Pope. Unless we have definite proof to the contrary, it is our Christian duty to presume that even those with whom we disagree are motivated by the sincerely held conviction that their own position is the right one. This in no way conflicts with what I wrote concerning "doublethink" on p. 14. The essence of "doublethink" is that the person employing it *knows* that black is white.

## Minorities can be Right

At the same time, no traditionalists should be distressed at being in a minority. Within this country practicing Catholics form a minority of only 3.6 per cent of the population — which in no way reflects upon the credibility of Catholicism.[63] Even if traditionalists formed an equally small minority within the Church they could still be right. It is worth remembering what Cardinal Newman wrote in his sermon *The Second Spring*, concerning the remnant of Catholics who remained faithful during penal times. They were:

"...but a few adherents of the Old Religion, moving silently and sorrowfully about, as memorials of what had been. 'The Roman Catholics'; — not a sect, not even an interest as men conceived it...but merely a handful of individuals, who might be counted, like the pebbles and *detritus* of the great deluge...found in corners, and alleys, and cellars, and the housetops, or in the recesses of the country; cut off from the populous world around them, and dimly seen as if through a mist or in twilight, as ghosts

43

flitting to and fro, by the high Protestants, the lords of the earth."[64]

Writing in the Canadian *Catholic Register* on 1 October 1977, Bishop G. Emmet Carter professed to explain the "real issue behind Lefebvre". As a convenient method of avoiding the actual arguments put forward by Archbishop Lefebvre, Bishop Carter remarked: "He has decided that the legitimately elected pope and the validly ordained bishops of the Universal Catholic Church are wrong. He has decided that he, Marcel Lefebvre, is 'right *envers et contre tous'* (against all comers)."

The same could have been said of St. Athanasius, who underwent the agony of having his excommunication confirmed by the Pope when he stood *contra mundum* — against the world. But there were some bishops who supported St. Athanasius and there are a good number today who support Msgr. Lefebvre in private. I have recently received a letter from an Archbishop thanking me for my defense of Msgr. Lefebvre in the first pamphlet in the present series. But what the words of Bishop Carter brought most vividly to my mind was a passage from *Nineteen Eighty-Four*: "Being in a minority, even in a minority of one, did not make you mad. There was truth and there was untruth, and if you clung to the truth even against the whole world, you were not mad."[65]

### The Fort is Betrayed

What this pamphlet should have made clear is that an important faction among the bishops at Vatican II wished to remove all obstacles preventing reunion with Protestants; that Protestant observers played an important part in the Council itself and in the *Consilium* which produced the *Novus Ordo Missae*; that the *Novus Ordo Missae* was defined as a Protestant service and can be officially celebrated in such a manner that not only Anglicans but Evangelical Protestants feel at home with it and consider that its theology conforms to Protestant norms: that although Article 7 has been changed, the form of Mass which it so accurately described, has not; that there is co-operation between our own Church and at least the Church of England in working towards a common service which will eventually be acceptable to nonconformists; and that our liturgy is still evolving and the evolution is taking a direction which removes it ever farther from the theology of the Council of Trent and ever closer to the theology of the Reformation. During the course of the Council Fr. Edward Schillebeeckx remarked: "One is astounded to find oneself more in sympathy with the thinking of Christian, non-Catholic 'observers' than with the views of one's own brethren on the other side of the dividing line. The accusation of connivance with the Reformation is therefore not without foundation. What is, in fact, happening then?"[66]

What indeed?

Protestants have good cause to rejoice at what has happened. One Lutheran theologian has summed it up as follows:

"Though some criticisms remain necessary and though some *desiderata* remain to be accomplished, those not (yet) united with the Latin Church may say, *gratias agamus Domino Deo nostro.*"[67]

Given the accuracy of the assessment set out in this pamphlet the only appropriate reply which a Catholic can make to the question posed by Father Schillebeeckx is to quote the words used by St. John Fisher of his apostate colleagues:

✓ "The fort is betrayed even of them that should have defended it."

## POPE PAUL VI WITH
## THE SIX PROTESTANT OBSERVERS

The photograph, taken on 10 April 1970, and published in issue 1562 of *La Documentation Catholique*, 3 May 1970, shows the Holy Father with, from left to right: Drs. George, Jasper, Shepherd, Kunneth, Brand, and to the right of Paul VI, Max Thurian.

# APPENDIX

*The Participation of the Protestant Observers in the compilation of the new Catholic liturgical texts.*

On 3 May 1970 *Documentation Catholique* published the text of a speech made by Pope Paul VI to the members of the *Consilium*, the body responsible for implementing the very generalized principles of liturgical reform included in the Liturgy Constitution of Vatican II. I have shown in *Pope John's Council* the extent to which this reform not only failed to correspond with the revisions envisaged by the Council Fathers but that it is in formal contradiction with both the Liturgy Constitution and the papally-approved liturgical movement. The cover of this issue of *Documentation Catholique* was devoted to a picture of Pope Paul VI posing with the six Protestant Observers who had been invited to participate in the work of the *Consilium*. This photograph proved to be a source of astonishment and even scandal to large numbers of the faithful who had no idea that Protestants had played any part in the compilation of the new Catholic rites. This resulted in public controversy in a number of countries followed by official denials that the Observers had, in fact, played any part in the compilation of the new rites. These denials have since been cited by apologists for the official reform as "refutations" of the allegation that Protestant Observers had taken an active part in the compilation of the new rites. There is, however, a considerable difference between a denial and a refutation, and these particular denials are totally gratuitous and contradict the available evidence.

In the July/August 1974 issue of *Notitiae*, official journal of the *Consilium*, Archbishop Bugnini (its secretary) claimed that the Observers confined their role simply to observing (pp. 249/50). Here are his exact words:

"What role did the 'Observer' play in the *Consilium*? Nothing more than that of — 'observer'. First of all they

47

only took part in the study meetings. In the second place they behaved with impeccable discretion. They never intervened in the discussions and never asked to speak."

On 25 February 1976 the Director of the Vatican Press Office gave the following reply to a question by the journalist George Huber as to whether the Protestant Observers had participated in the elaboration of the new Mass:

"The Protestant Observers did not participate in the elaboration of the texts of the new Missal."

This denial was printed in *Documentation Catholique* on 4 July 1976.

In contrast with this Msgr. W.W. Baum (now Cardinal Baum), an ardent ecumenist, made the following statement in a personal interview with the *Detroit News* on 27 June 1967:

"They are not simply there as observers, *but as consultants as well*, and they *participate fully* in the discussions on Catholic liturgical renewal. It wouldn't mean much if they just listened, *but* they contribute." (My emphasis.)

In order to place this statement in its correct context it must be made clear that, at the time he made it, Msgr. Baum was executive director of the American Catholic Bishops' Commission on Ecumenical Affairs, and the first Catholic spokesman ever invited to address the General Synod of the United Church of Christ, an American Protestant denomination. During his address he revealed to the delegates that Protestant scholars "have had a voice" in the revision of the Catholic liturgy. As a follow-up to this revelation, Harold Acharhern, Religious Correspondent of the *Detroit News*, obtained the interview with Msgr. Baum from which I have quoted.

The account given by Cardinal Baum, and the denials issued by Archbishop Bugnini and the Vatican Press Office are clearly contradictory. In order to discover the truth I wrote to one of the Observers, Canon Ronald Jasper. Before giving his reply it is necessary to explain the manner in which the *Consilium* did its work. Firstly, there were the study sessions during which the practical details of the reform were worked out, discussed, and modified. Then there were the formal (plenary) meetings during which the draft services which had been compiled in the study sessions were debated and voted upon. In my letter to Canon Jasper I explained that I was working upon a series of books on the liturgical reform and that I particularly wished to know whether the Observers had had a voice in the formulation of the new rites of Mass and Ordination. In his reply, dated 10 February 1977, he explained that the Observers received all the documents from the drafters of the new service in the same way as did other members of the *Consilium*. They were then present at the debates when they were presented by the experts and debated by the *Consilium*, but the Observers were not allowed to join in the debate.

In the afternoon, however, Canon Jasper continued, they always had an informal meeting with the *periti* who had prepared the draft services, and at these meetings they were certainly allowed to comment and criticize and make suggestions. It was then for the *periti* to decide whether any of the Observers' points were worth taking up when the general debates in the *Consilium* were resumed. But, he concludes, these informal meetings were a complete free-for-all, and there was a very frank exchange of views.

Exactly the same process took place during the course of Vatican II. The Protestant Observers, while not allowed to speak in the plenary sessions, were able to take an active part in the informal discussions where the real work of drafting the documents was done. Their influence is visible in the finalized documents themselves. Evidence of this is provided in Chapter IX of *Pope John's Council*.

In addition to this evidence the testimony of Archdeacon Pawley cited on p. 19 is extremely relevant, as are some revelations made by Robert McAfee Brown, another of the Protestant Observers. He states that:

"Particularly during the discussion on ecumenism, it was apparent that many bishops wanted to know what Protestant reactions were to statements in the *schema* about Protestantism, and wanted to elicit Protestant opinions on how the *schema* could be improved. Thus, although we had no direct 'voice' on the Council floor, we did indeed have an indirect voice through the many contacts that were possible with the fathers and their indispensable strong right arms, the *periti*."[68]

Mr. McAfee Brown also reveals that there were occasions when the observers were able to have a direct "voice" on the Council floor. "Is there anything you Observers want said on the Council floor about *De Oecumenismo*?" one bishop asked.[69] The Observers then put their views in writing to be incorporated into written interventions made on their behalf by bishops.

Thus, although it could be argued that officially the observers played no part in drafting the conciliar documents, since they could neither vote nor speak in the debates, it is clear that they were able to influence the final format of these documents. This is precisely what took place with the formulation of the new liturgical rites by the post-conciliar *Consilium*.

# NOTES

1. Cited in N. Gihr's *The Holy Sacrifice of the Mass*, [St. Louis, 1908], p. 337; cf. *The Tridentine Mass* (Augustine Pamphlets, No. 2), pp. 19/20.
2. See: The *Universe* of 5 August 1977, p. 13, and also of 19 August 1977, p.8: the C.T.S. Pamphlet, *Light on Archbishop Lefebvre*, by Msgr. G.R. Leonard, Chief Information Officer of the Catholic Information Office of England and Wales, pp. 7-10: the C.T.S. pamphlet, *Liturgical Changes, The Background*, by Father J.D. Crichton, p. 9, where he says: "In spite of everything, the New Order of Mass is *not* new except in one or two minor details."
3. *lo Specchio*, 16 May 1969.
4. *The Tablet*, 15 February 1964, p. 195.
5. *The Tablet*, 14 August 1965, p. 914.
6. *Emmanuel*, October 1975, p. 419.
7. *The Ampleforth Journal*, Summer 1971, p. 55.
8. *Demain La Liturgie* (Paris, 1976), pp. 9-10.
9. *Des Sacraments et des Hommes* (Paris, 1977), p. 34.
10. *The Decomposition of Catholicism* (London, 1970). p. 99.
11. Ibid.
12. *Religieux et Clercs contre Dieu* (Aubier, 1975), p. 12.
13. See *Pope John's Council*, Appendix VIII.
14. *The Christian Challenge*, February 1975, p. 15.
15. *The Clergy Review*, April 1975 (Editorial).
16. Francis Clark, *Eucharistic Sacrifice and the Reformation* (Oxford, 1967), p. 194.
17. *Cranmer's Godly Order*, p. 91.
18. *The Tablet*, 12 March 1966, p. 297.
19. *Nineteen Eighty-Four* (Penguin edition), p. 170.
20. Ibid, p. 197.
21. *The Tablet*, 25 October 1975, p. 1040.
22. *Notitiae*, No. 92, April 1974, p. 126.
23. *The Tablet*, 15 January 1966, p. 71.
24. *A Vindication of the Bull Apostolicae Curae* (London, 1898), p. 54.
25. *The Teaching of the Catholic Church*, G. Smith (London, 1956), p. 1056.
26. Op. cit., Note 24, pp. 43-44.
27. *A Bishop Speaks*, p. 15. (Available from Scottish Una Voce, 6 Belford Park, Edinburgh, EH4 3DP at L1.30 post inc. Readers in the U.S.A. should order from *The Remnant*, 2539 Morrison Ave., St. Paul, Minn., 55117 at $4.50, post inc.)
28. *L'Osservatore Romano* (English edition), 14 June 1973, p. 8.
29. *Rome and Canterbury through Four Centuries* (London, 1974), p. 343.
30. *Vatican Observed* (London, 1967), p. 47.
31. Rev. A. Abbott, S.J. (Editor). *The Documents of Vatican II* (London, 1967), pp. 179 & 181.
32. Xavier Rynne, *Letters From Vatican City* (New York, 1963), p. 115.
33. Rev. R.M. Wiltgen, *The Rhine Flows Into the Tiber* (New York, 1967), p. 242.
34. *General Instruction of the Roman Missal*, Article 242.
35. Op. cit., Note 32, pp. 111-12.
36. *The Tablet*, 16 September 1972, p. 893.

37. See *Cranmer's Godly Order*, pp. 95-98.
38. *The Tidings*, 9 July 1971.
39. *Christian Order*, October 1976, pp. 596-597.
40. Included in *A Sharp Critique* (of the New Mass), available from Scottish Una Voce at 20p., post inc.
41. For a detailed list of the prayers which Cranmer removed from the Sarum rite, see *Cranmer's Godly Order*, Chapter XII. For an examination of the importance of the *Suspice Sancte Pater*, see *The Tridentine Mass*, pp. 21-22.
42. Fr. Anthony Boylan, Secretary of the Liturgical Commission of England and Wales, *The Catholic Fireside*, 8 June 1973. See also Archbishop Bugnini, *Notitiae*, July/August 1974, p. 249. In this issue of *Notitiae* the Rev. Eugene L. Brand is listed as one of the observers but not Dr. Smith as cited in *La Documentation Catholique*. The gist of the *Notitiae* article was cited in *The Tablet* of 21 September 1974 by Fr. J.D. Crichton. He did so again in the *Catholic Herald* of 15 August 1975.
43. *The Catholic Standard* (Dublin), 14 September 1973.
44. *The Catholic Fireside*, 8 June 1973.
45. *Catholic Herald*, 1 August 1975.
46. *Catholic Herald*, 22 December 1972.
47. *Catholic Herald*, 15 December 1972.
48. *Le Monde*, 22 November 1969.
49. *La Croix*, 10 December 1969
50. *L'Osservatore Romano*, 13 October 1967, p. 3.
51. *The Clergy Review*, July 1973, p. 544.
52. *English Churchman*, 18 June 1976, p. 4.
53. *Concilium*, February 1969, p. 52.
54. *L'Eglise en Alsace*, January 1974.
55. *Pilgrim from Canterbury*, Atonement Fathers (Garrison, N.Y., 1972), p. 20.
56. *The Modern Mass* (Devon, 1969), p. 23.
57. *The Great Betrayal* (Devon, 1970), p. 26.
58. H.C. Schmidt-Lauber in *Emmanuel*, September 1975, p. 508.
59. *Studia Liturgica*, vol. 11, 1976, No. 2, p. 104.
60. Op. cit., note 58.
61. *Newsletter* of the Bishops' Committee on the Liturgy, vol. XII, September 1976.
62. Cited in *Cranmer's Godly Order*, p. 55.
63. See *Social Trends*, No. 7 (H.M.S.O., 1976).
64. See *Cranmer's Godly Order*, p. 139, for a longer extract from this sermon.
65. Op. cit., Note 19, p. 173.
66. *Catholic Gazette*, January 1964, p. 6.
67. Op. cit., Note 58, p. 509.
68. *Observer in Rome* (Methuen 1964), pp. 227-228.
69. Ibid, p. 173.

# INDEX

## A

The Agreed Statement
on Ministry and Ordination..............36
*Ampleforth Journal*.....................5
The Anglican Association......................30
*Apostolicae Curae,* a vindication......17,18
Armstrong, Canon C.B. .........................30

## B

Bacci, Cardinal..........................26
Baum, Cardinal W. ...........................47
Bouyer, Rev. L. .................................7,42
Boylan, Father A...............................28
Brown, R. McAfee..............................49
Bugnini, Archbishop.........16,28,42,46,47

## C

*Canterbury Agreement*............................35
Carter, Bishop G. Emmet..................14,44
*Catholic Gazette* .....................................32
*Catholic Herald*...........................28,29,36
*Catholic Register,* Canada ................14,44
Celada, Msgr. D. ....................................4
Charley, Dr. J.W. .........................35,36,40
Church of the
Confession of Augsburg...................34
Church of South India............................41
Clark, Rev. F. ...................................17
*Clergy Review*.......................................9
*Concilium* .............................................32
The *Consilium*.....22,23,26,27,29,44,46-49
*Constitution of the Liturgy*...............21,22
Cranmer .......................12,17,26,27,40,42
*Cranmer's Godly Order*...............12,38,42
Crichton, Rev. J.D. .................14,24,26,28
*La Croix*................................................34
Cullmann, O. .........................................19

## D

Denis, Rev. H......................................7
*Documentation Catholique*.....22,23,46,47
Dwyer, Archbishop R.J......................22

## E

*English Churchmen*..............................30

## G

Gardiner, Bishop......................................17
Gelineau, S.J., Rev. J. .........................6,15
Godfrey, Cardinal..............................20,35

George, Dr. .............................................22
*The Great Terror*....................................*11*
Greeley, Rev. A. ......................................9
Guitton, Jean ........................................30

## H

Hallinan, Archbishop .............................5
Heenan, Cardinal .............................5,21
Houghton, Rev. B. ................................24
Howell, Fr. Clifford .............................24

## I

ICET.......................................................33

## J

Jasper, Canon R. .....................22,29,47,48

## K

Küng, Hans ............................................35
Kunneth, Dr. .........................................22

## L

Lefebvre, Archbishop M..............18,37,44
Liturgical Changes–the Background .....14
Lucey, Bishop ........................................27
Luther, Martin ...................................19,42

## M

Madiran, Jean.....................................22,24
Mass attendance ......................................9
Moorman, Bishop ..................................19
*Music and Liturgy* ................................33

## N

Newman, Cardinal ............................17,43
*Nineteen Eighty-Four.*.................14,15,44
*Novus Ordo Missae*........4,22,24,26,27,30,
34,35,40,44

## O

Orthodox Church ....................................21
Ottaviani, Cardinal.................................26

## P

Paul VI, Pope .............5,15,22,24,26,30,46
Pawley, Archdeacon.....................19,36,48
Pelikan, Dr. J.....................................19,20
Prayerbook of Edward VI.....................17

## R

Ramsey, Archbishop of Canterbury.......37

Ross Williamson, H. ..........................37,41

**S**

St. Athanasius ............................. .............44
St. John Fisher ........................................45
St. Pius V, Pope.......................... 3,4,15,26
Schillebeeckx, Fr.................................20,45
Shepherd, Dr. ..........................................22
Siegvalt, M.G............................................29
Smith, Canon ..........................................18
Smith, Dr. D.............................................22
Southwark, Bishop of .............................29
Stacey, Rev. D...........................................32
Sykes, C. .................................................12

**T**

*The Tablet*................................................ 17
Thurian, Brother Max ........................22,34
Transignification .....................................37

**U**

Uniate Church ........................................21
*The Universe* ..........................................36

**W**

Waterhouse, S.J., Rev. H.O. ...................30
Waugh, Evelyn......................................5,10
*Windsor Agreement on the Eucharist* ....35
Wiseman, Cardinal....................................3
Woodruff, D...................... ................. 14
World Council of Churches ....22,24,32,37